Investing In Stocks

A Guide for Investing Safely

Table of Contents

Introduction 1

Chapter 1. Determining Risk Tolerance 3

Chapter 2. Investment Options 14

Chapter 3. Strategies for Safe Investment 31

Chapter 4. Entering the Market Step-By-Step 43

Chapter 6. Glossary 73

Postscript 81

Introduction

Wall Street has a reputation for being a fast-paced, cutthroat place where fortunes are made and lost in a second. This can make it really intimidating for someone looking to invest who isn't interested in losing their shirt! While movies and television have painted the stock market as a dangerous place, there are plenty of investments and strategies that allow you invest safely. Even with no investing experience, following the steps in this book will guide you through the process of building a portfolio in a secure, measured way.

Some of the themes you'll encounter repeatedly in this book are diligence, patience, and research. These might not have the same appeal as guts or instincts, but they are more realistic and reliable building blocks to successful investing. Nobel Prize-winning economist Paul Samuelson said, "Investing should be more like watching paint dry or watching grass grow. If you want excitement, take $800 and go to Las Vegas." He was right. It pays to remember that the reason for entering the market is not for kicks, but for your future.

In other words, investing in stocks should be considered from the standpoint of a compounding process—this means that instead of dashing into trades that promise, on the surface, to be profitable, you will exercise caution, patience, and diligence to let your profits, no matter how small they are, compound over a certain period of time. This book is written for the purpose of simplifying stock investing for you. When you finish this book you'll be ready to buy your first stocks and start building a portfolio. Let's dig right in and start putting together the knowledge base that will allow you to do that safely.

Chapter 1. Determining Risk Tolerance

The first step in building your portfolio is determining how much risk and what kind of risk you are willing to accept in order to meet your financial goals. Any investment comes with some risk. Some "experts" will tell you that high-return, no-risk investment options exist, but it isn't true, and anyone who says so is selling something. Risk isn't evil, though, and it can be managed in a secure way. In order to do that, you'll first have to decide what level of overall risk you're willing to accept. There are different kinds of risks, but the most common type is financial risk. Before putting your hard-earned money on stocks, you may want to ask yourself the following questions: What level of financial risks am I comfortable with? Will my life and that of my loved ones be affected if I unexpectedly suffer huge loses? Several factors must be considered when determining the risk tolerance in your portfolio. Let's take a look at them:

Age

The old rule of thumb is, "Subtract your age from 100 to find the percentage of your portfolio that should be comprised of stocks." So, if you were 40 years old, 60% of your holdings should be equities and the other 40% should be made of "safer" investments like savings bonds or real estate. While this can work for some people, it isn't a magic bullet. Age is only part of the picture. While it's true that the younger you are, the more time you'll have to recover if a risky investment doesn't pan out, some older investors are also willing to take on more risk. Conversely, depending on circumstance, a young investor may be wary of holding too much risk. Some tipsters have modified the adage to, "Subtract your age from 110 (or 125)…" to allow for more risk. That's all well and good, but it really makes more sense to make your decisions on where you are in your life rather than a raw formula.

More current wisdom is that all portfolios should hold a fair amount of equities throughout the investor's lifetime. This doesn't mean that everyone is going to be a day-trading adrenaline junkie, just that when chosen correctly, stocks can be safe at any time of one's life.

Another way to put this idea is that when you are investing in stocks, what are your long-term aspirations? If you aim at retiring finally at the age of 60, and you are somewhere between 30 and 45 years old now, you should be anxious to have in your portfolio equities that will mature over a long period of time. This is in sharp contrast to day-trading, whereby a trader hopes to capitalize on sudden price movements to lock in gains, no matter how small or big they are. Though, this may not be true for all cases, traders who are well advanced in age mostly pay attention to the size and length of their exposure to risks. Younger players are mainly powered by adrenalin that seems to be greed-fueled when investing in stocks; they are not afraid to stake everything they had got on a very promising position. Experienced traders rarely do that; they believe in the proverbial saying that "one should never put all his/her eggs in one basket". George Soros, the aged and renowned fund manager, reportedly once said that he is not always in the market. But whenever he spotted a great opportunity, he would bet "the whole village" on it. With his patience, Soros may end up making very few investments in a year, but unlike many nervous and unsettled day traders, he scored more profits by investing at the right time on the right equities.

It may be scientifically difficult to prove this, but fund managers who are matured and advanced in age are, eventually, some of the most successful ones. This may be due, in part, to their patience, diligence, and risk-averse tendency. These include George Soros, Bill Gross, Stanley Druckenmiller, Paul Tudor Jones and so on. Younger traders who made name for themselves in the 80s and 90s have, in one way or the other, lost their fortune and went bankrupt or scaled back the sizes of their portfolios.

Goals

Knowing why you're investing will guide your investments more than any other single factor. Before you even look at your first stock, sit down and make a timeline of your goals. If you are planning to start a business in five years, or retire in ten, that will have a huge effect on the amount of risk you should accept. Other key questions you should ask yourself are: How much money do I stand to make from this investment (my expected returns)? How much of my money would be tied up in inaccessible funds (restrictions on trading capital)? And how much will I able to withdraw at any given time (Is there any withdrawal limit)?

Your investment goals can also reveal your risk appetite. If you are targeting a "safe fund" in a decade or two, you will not be in the position to constantly day-trade or frequently tamper with your portfolios. You will rather choose to invest in value, snapping up stocks that have sustained profitability over a long time.

It is not new that people poured their resources on stocks and other equities for the purpose of settling some financial concerns in the future. People bought stocks to save funds for their children's education, wedding, or for purchasing fixed property, cars, or even for their own funeral. With a plan in mind, you will be very selective about which stocks to buy and which ones to avoid. No astute trader wants to have a basket of very volatile stocks in his/her portfolios when he/she is planning to cash in on them 20 to 30 years from now. For those with little or no investing/trading experience, there are countless financial advisors out there who might promise to help them draw up effective investment/financial goals. While this approach may be helpful to some extent, risk-taking tendencies should be based on personal decisions. You are the only person who fully understands your risk appetite. Several people have complained about losing grips on their investment strategies as they allowed all vital decisions to be made by their financial advisor (s). This is the reason we have many disgruntled stock investors who are always quick to discourage other people from putting their hard-earned money into stock trading. You should be able to state clearly your expected risks, and devise mechanisms to deal with the aftermath of such an investment plan. The absence of a well-planned risk management is responsible for the many unsatisfactory stock-trading experiences we have today. Another simple way to put this important fact is that: If your risk appetite is just at the level of $500, you will not be doing yourself any good to follow the advice of a financial advisor that urges you to stake more than that on a stock investment. To maximize your profit-making possibility, you must stick to your initial investment goal that puts you within your circle of risk appetite.

Depth of Investment Knowledge

It is also reasonable to place your risk-taking ability within the depth of your investment knowledge. What this statement means is that you shouldn't attempt to risk your hard-earned money on stocks or other investment options that you have very little or no knowledge of. No doubt, financial/investment advisors are helpful, but having no idea how an investment plays out may put you at a greater risk. Everyone who dabbles into stocks understands, from the onset, that there are some risks involved. The earlier you are aware of this important fact, the better your prospect of making money from your investments. Though, financial/investment advisors are there to lead you through your investment journey, it is more reasonable to know exactly what they are doing with your money. And there is no better way to accomplish this than acquiring some knowledge about how stock trading works.

As a matter of fact, your stock trading knowledge will guide you, to a certain degree, into making choices that could lead to more profitable trades. This is because novice traders or investors have always ended up losing a chunk of or all of their investment capital on their first try. When picking stocks, you can utilize your investment knowledge to decide on which stocks are less volatile and could produce encouraging profits either in the short- or long- run. People who don't know anything about the art of stock -picking/investment are often liable to losing money.

Other Income

Keeping your long- and short-term goals in mind, what other sources of income do you have available to help you meet them? This is important because it helps you understand if you can afford to have periods of time where your stocks aren't paying dividends and still stay on track. Say, for example, you're saving up to retire. If your portfolio is your only retirement plan, you'll probably be less risk tolerant than someone who also has an IRA and 401(k). Either reality is fine as long as it's taken into account.

Your other sources or streams of income could also be investments in your own business or some other businesses. They could be some tangible properties such as real estate, yachts, parcel of land, or machinery. Knowing fully that your investment in stocks won't affect your financial future in a bad way may increase your appetite to take more risks. It is a bad decision to put all your resources into stocks when you apparently have nothing to fall back on in case things go awry, against all expectations. Stock-trading or investing is an unpredictable venture; you could lose all or a part of your investment. In the same way, it amounts to taking a foolish risk when all your future financial resources are tied up in very risky investment types.

Take for instance, it may not seem wise to put all your money on volatile stocks when you could have chosen to diversify your entire portfolios. Some smart investors will consider putting their hard-earned money in bonds, mutual funds as well as in some stocks. The idea is that if stock trades turn against you, you will still have some money left to re-invest or put away in savings.

Ability to Diversify

Ideally, every investor would start their stock market journey with enough money to fully invest in a wide range of assets. Unfortunately, that's not always the case. There is such a thing as "over-diversification," a term for when an investor is spread too thin. What happens in cases like this is that even if a number of stocks are very successful, not enough capital is invested, and the returns aren't appreciable.

As briefly discussed above, spreading your capital in various investments (of course, not spreading it too thin), can protect your portfolios from sudden market crashes or volatility. Sometimes winning in life is not all about knowing the right thing to do, but it is also about protecting yourself from disasters that may be typically out of your control. How can you stop a market crash? How can you hold a sway on the stock prices? How can you influence the technical and fundamentals that millions of traders worldwide use to make investment decisions? As you can see, the only brilliant thing you can do is to protect your investments from all these terrible, larger-than-life happenings!

When you diversify your investments, you are selectively choosing the level of risks you will want to be exposed to. This shows that you are approaching your investments like a soldier would: Offend and defend! You systematically launch your offensive at the market with the hope of profiting from it. Then you also cleverly cover your trades to save you from unsuspecting calamity.

Most people lose money while investing in stocks because they fail to realize that it is not what they know that matters, but how they smartly redistribute their risks.

How would you advise a person who has little savings and wishes to retire early? Would you ask him/her to put all his/her resources into one kind of investment? Or would you think it is much better if he/she spreads his\her assets across many investment types?

Put yourself in the same circumstance: If you are willing to protect your hard-earned resources, you will be patient to select investment options that will stay on for a long time, even into your retirement. The key is not to put one's investments in only one basket! It is very risky to do otherwise.

Chapter 2. Investment Options

Once you've decided on how much of your portfolio can be made up of equities, it's time to take a look at which equities will suit your needs. Not all investments are created equally, and if you're looking for less risky options, you may want to look at the ones that blend aspects of equities and savings instruments. Other safer options you can adopt to mitigate risk include bundling stocks, which provides automatic diversity. Or you can decide to go for stocks that pay dividends at a higher rate.

Highlighted below are different investment options that you can add to your portfolio. It is important to state that not all of them will be good for you: This is because some investments have various degrees of risks; while some, like bonds, are less risky, stocks and forex are very volatile and could lead to significant loss of investment (capital). As the saying goes in investor circles, that a savvy trader is the one who successfully protects his/her capital. Huge loss of capital may derail your investment goals.

Mutual Funds

Mutual funds are bundled investments that are overseen by a professional money manager. In any mutual fund, you'll find a hugely diverse range of stocks and other investments. One of the main benefits of a mutual fund is that since they are co-owned by so many people, the risk is spread out and therefore diluted. Obviously, the other side of that coin is that any returns are just as diluted. Another advantage of mutual funds is that because so many people contribute, the total amount of money able to be invested is very large. This can give you the opportunity to own very expensive (and worth it!) stock that otherwise would be out of reach. You will pay for this kind of buying power and the professional management that comes with a mutual fund: They all charge fees to buy in. Make sure that if you choose to invest in a mutual fund you know that its benefits will outweigh the costs.

Outlined below are five (5), main characteristics of a good mutual fund/mutual fund brokerage:

Low expenses: if your broker is charging expensive fees or collecting a huge percentage of your profits, run away from such a brokerage. The mutual fund returns are usually small because they have already been diluted. Imagine how negligible it would become if your broker is charging very high fees on performance.

Financially stable parent company: Choose a broker that has a strong parent company which is financially stable. This is a safety procedure to recoup your money in case something goes awry when least expected. Whenever there is a sudden, volatile swing in stocks and other securities, it is not new that some brokers encounter financial difficulties as their clients or customers lose a lot of money. A recent example was FXCM, a CFD firm that nearly went under when its clients placed huge bets of USDCHF that suddenly turned against them! The company wouldn't have survived this circumstance if not for its New York-based parent company that quickly sourced funds to remain in business.

Record of performance: Make sure you are using a brokerage that has good record of producing substantial yields. Though it is impossible to guess correctly whether current levels of performance can determine future returns. But a good rule of the thumb is to play safe and not get entangled with a poor-performing mutual funds brokerage.

Continuous investment processes: Go for a brokerage that is engaged in continuous investment processes. In other words, putting your hard-earned money in a brokerage that infrequently make investments across board may tie down your capital and bring no satisfactory returns at the end of the year. Ask to know some of the latest stocks and securities the brokerage has invested in, and analyze its performances accordingly.

The size of the fund: The main reason why the size of a fund matters is that the more capital the fund has at its disposal, the more investment opportunities it could be involved in. And it takes a widespread investment engagements to make any tangible profit in mutual funds.

It has also been broadly debated that mutual funds are good for investors who aim for long-term investments. Though the returns are small, but they could snowball or compound into something significant over a long period of time. This is why investors with low appetite for risks are advised to get aboard the mutual funds' trains.

It must be averred that there are some high-yield funds but, in general, most mutual funds become profitable when they are held for a long time.

Money Market Funds

A money market fund is a special type of mutual fund. They always seek to maintain a net asset value of $1 per share, which means that they pay dividends to when their value rises above that level. They are heavily comprised of short-term, low-risk investments like Treasury bills (T-bills), certificates of deposit (CDs) and corporate commercial paper, so they stay relatively liquid. This is good for investors who may need to move their money from one place to another quickly. For instance, if a stock in your portfolio begins to fall and you sell it, but don't immediately have another in mind to buy, it may be advantageous for tax or other reasons to invest it in a money market fund. When the right stock does come along and you're ready to buy, the money in the fund is easily accessible. Some money market funds charge fees, just like a mutual fund, but they tend to be lower. No matter how low the fee, though, make sure you know what it is. The amount of the fee in dollars is, of course, important, but also important is what percentage of your total return the fee is. Obviously, a $25 fee is a drop in the bucket if you're investing enough to make a $1000 return, but if you're only investing a small amount and seeing a commensurately small return it's a much bigger deal.

One major advantage of money market fund is that it has no loads—loads are fees charged mutual funds for entering and exiting the fund. It is also common that some money market funds also provide an opportunity for their clients to invest in municipal securities that are tax-exempt at the federal and/or state levels. In other words, they can protect their gains from both the federal and state taxes.

However, the main concern about money market funds is that they are not covered by Federal Deposit insurance. However, they are regarded as safe investments because they are still regulated under the Investment Company Act of 1940.

Following the financial crash of 2008 and subsequent crises, the U.S. Securities and Exchange Commission (SEC) made some new rules for money market fund managers to provide them more stability and balance. The new rules place strict restrictions on portfolio holdings and indicates the appropriate triggers for suspending redemptions and for requesting payment of liquidity fees. The rules likewise demand that fund managers use floating net asset value (NAV) instead of fixed $1 NAV. It is understandable that the floating NAV rules will not have serious impacts on investors who put their money in funds designated as retail market funds, but its introduction into a fund that hasn't utilized it before may lead to significant loss of capital.

Stock Options

Stock options are contracts that give the holder an option to buy or sell the underlying asset, but not an obligation to do so. Because the value of the option is derived from the value of the underlying stock, options are what is known as derivatives. There are two types of options for buyers: Call Options and Put Options. A call option works like this: 100 shares of a stock are bundled together, and the option to buy them for a specified price is sold for a premium. That price is known as the "strike price." If and when the value of the stock rises above the strike price, the holder of the option can choose to buy it for the strike price, or choose not to and let the option expire. The expiration date of the contract is decided upfront and will factor into your decision to purchase it or not. A put option works exactly the same way, but instead of paying a premium for the right to buy a stock the holder buys the right to sell it. This can be a little bit confusing, so let's look at an example of an imaginary option to make it clearer.

Let's say that you buy a call option of Widgets Inc stock for a premium of $500 with a strike price of $50 per share and an expiration 12 months from now. This means that if any time in the next year the price per share rises above $50, you can buy it and still only pay $50. In this example, say that the price rises to $80 at some point. You can now buy the 100 shares for $5000, meaning that you've made a profit of $2500 (the difference between the value of the stock and what you paid, minus the initial premium you paid for the option.) If the stock never reaches a value above the strike price, you can simply let the option expire. You'll be out the $500 premium, but that's still a much less risky investment than buying the stock outright would have been.

A call option works in the same way, but in the opposite direction. If you buy the call options for the Widgets Inc stock, but you expect the value of each share to drop over the next year, you can sell them for the strike price even though they aren't worth that price at the time of sale. This means that put options can protect you against loss by locking in a guaranteed sale price. The stock market at large definitely offers no such guarantee!

Many companies today give their employees stock options, popularly referred to as Employee Stock Option (ESO). ESOs offer the lucky employees the right to buy a certain quantity of the company shares at a predetermined price for a certain period of time. However, employee stock options are a bit different from exchange-traded options in the sense that they are not traded between investors on an exchange. And ESOs work in the same way as other stock options. Imagine a director of a company is given the right to purchase 2000 shares of the company at a strike price of $30 per share. The arrangement may require that 1,500 of the shares vest after 4 years, while the remaining 500 shares vest in 6 years. When ESOs vest, it means the employee has assumed absolute ownership of them. Companies give their good employees ESOs and space the period required for their vesting so that they can retain such useful employees.

Some IT companies and Fortune 500 companies use employee stock options to motivate, retain, and reward their employees.

Income Stocks (also known as "dividend stocks")

When a stock's share price rises, the money earned can be used to fortify the company and/or be paid out to the owners of the stock. This payout is known as a "dividend." Companies that pay regular dividends inspire confidence in investors because if they didn't have reasonable cash flow, they wouldn't have the money to pay the dividends. This becomes self-perpetuating because once a stock has a reputation for paying regular dividends the management is committed to maintaining that reputation. Beware of stocks that pay extraordinarily high dividends, though. When a dividend is well above the norm it could be because the company is trying to buy that good reputation without having the strong financial underpinning that earns it.

Income stocks, which are also called income investments include other categories of investments such as real estate, bonds, annuities, certificates of deposit, money market funds, real estate investment funds, and so on.

If your plan is to achieve quick capital appreciation through sudden increase in the price of your stocks, you should give income stocks a try. Though these kinds of stocks may help investors to quickly increase their capital size by aggressively buying and selling shares. However, they can be very risky; an unexpected decline in the stock price or sudden market selloffs or high taxes on short-term investments could threaten the health of your portfolio.

Recently, there are reports that some retirees are putting their retirement savings in dividend stocks. In some extreme occasions, some of these retirees even went ahead to bet 100% of their retirement savings on the expectation that the share price will go up. While it is not a bad idea to seriously consider any form of investment, but putting one's 100% on income stocks, which can be subjected to sudden, risky events, is indeed a wrong move. Another reason why people (both experienced investors and newbies) are rushing to dividend stocks lately is because of the promise of a fat dividend. For the fact that most companies don't pay dividends may make people to be desperate when they offered the chance of earning huge dividends. However, the red flag is that such companies offering big dividends may not be financially strong after all; they may just be baiting traders to put in their hard-earned money and watch it disappear!

DRIPs

The value of dividend stocks comes from the power of compounding. We're all familiar with compound interest- the process where earned interest becomes part of the principal wealth and interest is earned on it. Reinvesting dividends works in the same way. Instead of just stacking up dividends in a savings account, using them to buy more stock increases the amount of stock earning dividends, increasing the dividends received, and on and on. A Dividend Reinvestment Plan, or DRIP, takes dividends and automatically re-buys stock. They can be run by the company, a broker, or a money manager. DRIPs that are run by the stock-issuing company are of particular interest to the investor looking for security. Because there is no middle man, there are no brokerage fees for the repurchase, and sometimes the stock bought with dividends is offered at a discount. Since this is a stock you presumably were confident enough in to own, reinvesting in it and compounding your earnings over time in this way is a great way to increase profit without increasing risk.

Most DRIPs permit investors to buy shares at a reduced price and commission-free. Some do not allow reinvestments below $10. So, instead of receiving your dividends as a check or a direct deposit into your bank account, your money will be reinvested by the conditions stated in your DRIP. Since DRIPs are obtained from a company's share reserve, it is practically impossible to market these shares on stock exchanges. And you will only be able to redeem your shares through the company. If you cannot set up your DRIP directly with a company, you may decide to use a broker. In this case, the broker will be the go-between and activate the reinvestment.

Remember that even though you didn't receive your dividends in cash, you will still have to declare them on your tax forms, because they are taxable.

In general, outlined below are some advantages of DRIP:

- Commission-free reinvestments
- Possibility of being rich through compounding
- Financial security if the company one invested in succeeds
- Ability to purchase additional stocks with dividends at a discounted price
- Possibility of purchasing stocks in fractions if the company has a class of expensive stocks.

Common stocks

A common stock is a security that denotes an ownership in a business or a company. If you bought a company's common stocks, you are entitled to owning a part of its equity. This gives you the chance to control the company's operations through a voting right—you can elect a board of directors and vote on corporate policy.

The common stock is the most common kind of shares. A big part of stocks people bought over the counter or through exchanges are probably common stocks. In 2016, there are more than 4,000 stocks traded on major exchanges and more than 15,000 traded over the counter. This category of stocks can also be bought on the Over-The-

Counter Bulletin Board (OTCBB) or pink sheets, where small companies that do not meet the popular exchanges' listing requirements list their stocks.

Here are the features of the common stocks everyone must have knowledge of:

- The common stocks are less secure than preferred stocks or bonds.
- Common stockholders receive their dividends only after the preferred stockholders have been paid.
- In case the company you bought stocks from goes bankrupt, when redeeming funds, preferences will be given to people who invested in preferred stocks and bonds before common-stock holders can receive any settlement.
- As a result of this, common stocks can be considered to be somehow unsafe investment—one can lose all his/her investment in case the folded company couldn't source enough funds to liquidate its debts.

Preferred Stocks

Preferred stocks combine some of the aspects of debt ownership and equity ownership. They pay fixed, rather than variable dividends like a debt instrument. But they also can fluctuate in asset value like an equity. Owners of preferred stock are paid their dividends before common stockholders, so in times of trouble for the company or market, they're somewhat protected. The downside of this type of stock is that its value isn't as susceptible to market upturns or increases in company profits. Again, the correlation between risk and return is evident.

Described below are some characteristics of preferred stocks:

- Payment of dividends to preferred stockholders is compulsory, unlike common stockholders' condition
- Dividends can be paid monthly or quarterly
- However, a person owing preferred stocks do not have a voting right
- When the company collapses or is acquired, preference is given to preferred stock investors as far as repayment is concerned
- But preferred stocks do not correspondingly increase in value, unlike common stocks. This means that their prices hardly increase by a large percentage; they are usually a few dollars more than their initial price (up to $25). On the other hand, common stocks' prices can spike to any amount if the company's credit-worthiness suddenly improves.

- It is possible to convert some preferred stocks into common shares; and it is believed that preferred stockholders who haven't received their first dividends can exercise some voting rights.
- Preferred stocks, like bonds, are rated by the main rating companies like Moody's and Standard and Poor's.

Two kinds of stocks

Stocks can be classified based on their kinds. There are: (i) growth stocks; and (ii) value stocks.

(i) **Growth stocks:** When people talk of growth investing, it means they are buying shares in a company that is positioned to enjoy capital or earning growth in the succeeding periods. Take for instance, Apple, Inc has always maintained healthy capital growth; when people bought Apple's shares, they are expecting it to produce better earnings in each quarter.

(ii) **Value stocks:** Warren Buffet is the most popular example of a value investor. In other words, the Oracle of Omaha only puts his money on shares from companies he believes are valuable, and/or will increase their values in the succeeding periods. Value stocks are somehow overlooked or underrated stocks, but a shrewd investor knows that, judging by the quality of products or services offered by the company, the worth of its stocks will rise in the near future. Incidentally, most value stocks are undervalued, but if you are smart enough to identify those that can rise in value in the short- or long-term, you are on your way to becoming a profitable stock trader. Look around you, you will probably discover some products that are good but are somehow undervalued. Knowing fully well that the usefulness of such products may increase in the near future, that may prompt you to invest in the stocks of the companies that produce such products or services.

Chapter 3. Strategies for Safe Investment

No matter which individual investments you choose for your portfolio, there are general strategies you can use to protect yourself against loss. From the selection process to the methods you use to make trades to how you react to market volatility, some options are going to be safer than others. In this chapter, we'll look at ways to build security into your investment process without limiting your ability to generate income from it.

It has been shown that over-protection of your portfolio may also lead to poor returns, as the fear of losing your capital may discourage you from taking reasonable amounts of trades. Being moderate is also essential to remaining a profitable stock investor. The act of moderation will prevent you from over-trading or engaging in excessive stock-buying fueled by greed and adrenalin.

Diversification

This is probably the word you'll hear most as an investor, and it's easy to understand why. In an undiversified portfolio, not only can the fortune of one company make or break an investor, but missed opportunities are completely unavoidable. There are two kinds of diversification, and both are important. First, diversification of industry and stock type means that a healthy portfolio will hold stocks in a variety of sectors. For example, owning shares in real estate, pharmaceuticals, airlines, and utilities makes it very unlikely that all of your stocks will fall at the same time. This is the type of diversity that most investors are familiar with. The second type of diversity is diversity within sectors. This means not just picking one winner within the industry you invest in, but taking advantage of competition between companies.

We touched on this a little bit above, but it is possible to "over-diversify." A good rule of thumb is that no more than 10% of your investments should be in one place at the same time. When you're just starting out and your initial funds are limited, sticking close to this ratio is a good idea. As your portfolio grows you may invest more heavily in areas that are performing well for you.

The primary aim of buying stocks is to make some gains. And there is no better way to achieve that purpose than diversifying one's portfolio. These are three ways you can increase your investment returns through diversification:

- Spreading your risks across many holdings can help reduce losses in a way that some losses in some equities will be assuaged by the profits from the others.
- When buying shares from competitors, this action can expose you to some fundamentals of the rivals and give you an edge in making informed trade decisions.
- Diversification, when done appropriately, can significantly increase your gains while reducing the amount spent on fees. Using the same brokerage to acquire different types of equities can cut back on the amount of fees you should have paid for using different brokers.

On the other hand, the dangers of over-diversifications are that:

- Spreading your resources too thin can cause the volume of your profits or gains to be quite small and intangible
- Over-diversification in too many stocks can be time-consuming and confusing, leading to poor performance and little gains

This is why moderation is essential if you want to become a winning investor.

Put Options

In times of market downturn, put options provide a buffer. Let's say you see a stock that's risen unusually quickly, and you expect for it to drop back to a more expected, level price soon. Buying a put option with an expiration date of a few months and a strike price above what you expect it to drop to means that if that fall does occur, you'll make a profit from the sale.

Options can be used to reduce risks of investments: This is done through the concept of leverage. In other words, buying the options of underlying stocks may help you hedge against the unexpected or swift movement or volatility in those stocks. The amount you invested in options can offset any amount of loss you may have incurred in equivalent investment in the underlying stocks. Highlighted below are two unique ways options can act as a useful leverage for your investments:

(i) You can use options as a leverage to capture larger position than the equivalent investment you may have made on the underlying stocks. In essence, when you profit from the options, this can help you reduce the overall risks in your stock investments.

(ii) You can hold positions of the same size with options and stock trading; however, it is cheaper to maintaining options than holding similar size of stocks in one's portfolio.

To better illustrate the facts outlined above, if your initial plan is to invest $20,000 in a $100 stock, it may appear more sensible to you to rather invest $20,000 in $20 options. This is because you can control 1000 shares of the underlying stocks through options instead of 200 shares you may have got if you had invested directly on stocks.

There are two different types of **put options:**

(i) *Long put option:* If you are buying one put option of Apple (AAPL) stock with a strike price of $116, expiring in one month. In this case, you have the right to buy 100 shares of Apple at a price of $116 until the next month, which is the expiration date. However, if Apple share falls to $100 in the market and you choose to exercise your option, you can sell shares to the option's writer for $116 while buying new Apple shares for $100 each. As a result of this transaction, your profit can be calculated as thus: 100 x ($116-$100)

= 100 x 16 = **$1600.**

This calculation does not put into consideration the premium you paid to get the put option.

(ii) **Short put option:** This is direct opposite of long put option, because a short put option gives you the obligation to purchase shares of the underlying stocks. Imagine you are purchasing 100 Apple shares at a strike price of $116, and you have no idea that it will fall to $100 in the next two weeks. You can collect a premium by writing one put option on the Apple stock with a strike price of $100 for $3.5. So, you will collect (**100 x $3.5 =$350**) when the share closes above $100. However, if the share closes bellows $100, you are required to purchase 100 shares of Apple at $100 because of your contractual agreement!

LEAPS

This acronym stands for Long-Term Equity Anticipation Securities. These are very similar to call options, but they last for a much longer term. The risk of a call option is that the changes in price you're relying on won't happen in the limited amount of time before the option expires. Usually, the term of a call option is a few weeks or months. LEAPS typically last for a year or two before expiring, so there's much more time for the underlying business to recover from financial hardship or to grow from strengthening or changing their fundamentals. Options are not the simplest investment, so it's worth talking to an experienced financial advisor about any options you're interested in.

Most long-term traders or investors, that is, those who prefer to hold a position for a long time, normally go for LEAPS. This is because it affords them the unique opportunity of gaining prolonged exposure to trends. LEAPS discourage active management of portfolio; so, if you are holding down a LEAP, you do not have the chance of tampering with it at the release of every financial data or other fundamental analysis. It is also cheaper to own LEAPS, when compared with purchasing the underlying stocks. You can own LEAPS of individual stocks as well as that of equity indexes such as S & P 500, Dow Indices, and NASDAQ – 100.

Stop-Losses

A stop loss order is a directive to sell specified stock if the price of that stock drops below a certain level. One traditional piece of investing wisdom that still holds very true is that you should never let any asset fall more than 10% before selling it. Sentiment, fear, and pride often motivate investors to hold on to stocks that are bleeding money. The stock market doesn't have feelings, though, so letting yours control your decisions is always a bad idea. Stop loss orders are a way to avoid this trap and make sure no one investment drags your whole portfolio down.

Outlined below are some of the benefits of using a stop loss order:

- It limits the amount of loss you can incur on a trade or stock. Many newbies who dabbled into stock investment often lose a chunk or all of their capital due to their failure to use a stop loss. Think of it this way: You are driving a car down the hill, and the only way you could reduce the impact of an accident is to apply the brakes somewhere down the slope. Without a stop loss order, you are just coursing down the slope and, if care is not taken, that may land you at the bottom of the hill, in a dangerous swamp--A complete wipe out of your investment capital!
- Stop loss order will give you the freedom to trade without any worry. In other words, you don't have to keep checking your trades every now and then. Active portfolio management is one of the factors responsible for having little profit because instead of letting your winning trades run, you will suddenly cut them short and take

small profits, fearing that you might lose the small profits already gained.

- Experienced stock traders understand the pattern of a chart or the trend of a security. For instance, they know how far a stock can swing at a particular period. Take for instance, consumer product and retail stocks move a lot during the end-of-the-year sales. As a result of this, you can use the stop loss to lock in some profit at a pre-selected price.
- If you are very emotional while trading, it is advisable that you use stop losses a lot. By doing so, you will be able to remove emotions from your trading and let your profits accumulate.
- Once you have been able to successfully build using "stop loss" into your strategy, you will get better over time in applying it to your trades.

The **only** disadvantage of using a stop loss is that it could work against you during highly volatile trading sessions. Even though you have properly done your analysis and have put up your stop loss at the appropriate place on the trade, you could be unluckily stopped out by huge swings that usually come from the volatility. This is why you should pay attention to timing.

There are no fast or hard rules for applying stop losses to your trades. You will get used to the strategy as you continuously apply it in your trading. However, putting a stop loss very close to your market order is not helpful—you will soon be stopped out. A rule of the thumb, as accepted by many traders, is that you should let your stop loss order stay, at least, 10 pips from your market order. Some long-term stock traders with huge capital can even put their stop loss orders at about 500 or 1000 pips from their market orders. Do not imitate those experienced traders; they could afford to do that because they are investing huge amount of money on their trades.

Selling Strategically

Selling, in general, is sometimes seen by rookie investors as a sign of failure, but this couldn't be further from the truth. Every experienced investor knows it is necessary and vital to shuck stock that isn't making you money. There will be times when you need to sell a stock, but don't have another purchase in mind to take its place. Buying bonds and CDs at that point can be a way to keep your money relatively liquid while still providing a return. A famous investing maxim is that "no one ever got rich with their money in a savings account." Making sure that you have somewhere to park your money between investments that still earns a respectable return is important. That leads us to a common practice on Wall Street and in every other place where stock trading takes place: "Short Selling". The concept of short selling is that some investors basically specialize in the art of selling stocks to lock in huge profits. Some of the famous short sellers in the history of stock trading include people like Jesse Livermore, George Soros, Bill Ackman, Daniel Loeb, Hempton, David Einhorn, and so on.

What investors do when they "short sell" is that they borrow a stock, sell it and then purchase the stock back at a lower price and return it to the lender. As a short seller, you may target any company whose shares you think are overvalued. This indicates that by selling the company's shares, you expect their prices to fall within a certain period of time.

Professional "short sellers" are considered the "enemies" of corporations. The reason is that a company that falls under aggressive short-selling may have its cashflow dried up and go bankrupt.

Even though short selling is allowed in the United States, it is forbidden in France and some other countries. For instance, when Bill Ackman attacked Herbalife and aggressively sold its share some years ago, the company was put under pressure that resulted in the immediate change in the company's management structure.

While short selling seems simple, but newbie investors must be careful in engaging in the practice, because they may lose their investment capital. It is mainly reserved for sophisticated investors, because a lot of capital is involved. And you must be versed in both fundamental and technical expertise to precisely predict or speculate that a company's stock value was going to decline because of overvaluation. Three factors that could move you to strategically sell your shares are:

- Learning that the stock market is going to tank—when there is a sudden event like a war or financial instability in some areas of the world, it would soon spread to the United States
- A change in leadership
- Bad reputation for the company you own its shares—maybe when their products or services fail. At this time, the company may lose a large part of its customer base and its revenue will drop significantly

If you keep holding on to the stocks of a company that are confronted with the three issues described above, you may end up biting your fingers in regret as you watch your hard-earned money disappear through poor trading choice.

Chapter 4. Entering the Market Step-By-Step

Now that you know how to choose investments and how to handle them, it's time to get into the logistics of buying stock. Fortunately, the internet has made this much more accessible than in the past. Luckily, the days of yelling to your broker over the phone are over, and you can handle every part of the investing process online. This chapter will guide you through, step-by-step, and give you the tools you need to make secure choices there.

Assessing Your Finances

Taking a hard and honest look at your current financial state is important for two reasons. First, you can't start investing until you know how much you have to invest. Second, before you start taking even limited risks with your capital you need to be sure your financial house is in order. Make a budget, track your spending, and ensure that if your investments perform more poorly than you expect you'll still be able to fund your life. If you have extensive debt, it's probably wiser to pay it down to manageable levels before you begin investing.

Once you've done this, you'll be able to come up with a hard figure representing what you can afford to invest. Break this number down quarterly. You'll need to re-address your finances at least this often, so it's convenient to have that figure.

Depending on the platform or broker you are using, there are some tools that could help you assess your financial strength in order to gauge your risk exposure. You may want to know the answers to these important questions before investing your hard-earned capital: How many shares can I purchase with my current capital? How much gains can I make from the investment? What is the expected performance of the stock?

The best approach to doing this is to calculate your risk and reward. If you cannot find the tool to estimate your risk and reward on your platform, and cannot obtain the service free of charge from your broker, you can follow these simple steps:

- Deeply research different stocks and pick one that you will like to invest in
- Go ahead and set the upward and downward price targets, considering the current price
- Calculate the risk/reward

- If the estimated risk/reward is below your expected ratio, you can raise your downside price target
- But if you can arrive at a good risk-to-reward ratio, you can start all over again with another investment idea

Normally, the widely-used risk: reward ratio is 1:2, meaning that you expected to make twice the amount of capital you have put into your stock investment. You can always adjust the target prices to achieve your desired or expected ratio. While it is a good feeling to double one's investment (using 1:2 ratio), but in reality, the most common ratios somehow hover between 1:1 and 1: 1.5.

There are other financial calculation tools that can help you estimate the "margin", "leverage", and "investment lots (sizes)".

Choosing a Stock or Fund

Obviously, this is a complicated decision, but the basic steps to choosing a stock don't change. Take these tips as a starting point to your decision-making process and add in your own experience and wisdom as you gain them. It's particularly important to not let "hot tips" or "gut feelings" taint your decision-making at this stage. There is real information that can guide you, so focus on that and ignore the extraneous noise. The four steps below will give you a solid base with which to make your choices:

(i) ***Industry-based search:*** It is natural for people to look for stock investment in the industry they have knowledge of or in which they have had some success in the past. Investors who had made good money in tech stocks will stick to that industry; likewise, if your first big gains had come from the financial or pharmaceutical industry, you will not want to take any risk of trying out stocks from other industries.

(ii) ***Analyzing the company's statistics:*** Once you have chosen which industry to invest in, the next thing to do is to select a company to buy shares from. Of course, there are going to be many companies in the same industry. You may have decided on a couple of companies in your chosen industry, however, extended analysis is required before settling down on one company. You may want to determine the following attributes of the company before finally jumping on the bandwagon to purchase its shares:

- Determine the company's market capitalization or valuation, assets, book value, earnings (both the current and projected ones)
- Estimate its value or growth capabilities

- Determine or calculate its debt ratio, liquidity ratio, profitability ratio using common ratios such as Price-to-earning (P/E), Price-to-sales (P/S), price-to-book (P/B), enterprise value to earnings before interest, taxes, depreciation, and amortization (EV/EBITDA). On most occasions, all these pieces of information highlighted above can be obtained from the company's Annual Report.

(iii) **Screening:** Having obtained the pertinent information listed above about a few companies, the next step is to screen them based on your personal criteria. For example, you may want to invest in a company with the following characteristics:

- High revenue growth
- Huge market capitalization
- Mature industry
- High profitability and liquidity
- Less debt profile

Remember that a company that fulfils all your requirements may have expensive shares. So, some compromises are required for you to find a stock that is affordable as well as profitable. You will surely get better at stock-picking after scoring your first gains in the process. It doesn't matter how long it will take you to settle down on a company's stock, what is the most important aspect of this process is that you make an informed choice that you will not regret about later.

(iv) **_Purchasing the stock/investing in the Fund:_** You should go ahead and purchase your stock or invest in your chosen fund. Don't forget that some companies have different classifications of stocks. Take for instance, Warren Buffet's Berkshire Hathaway has two classes of stocks: Class A, which is more expensive than the Class B. It costs about $250,000 to buy just one share of Berkshire Hathaway's Class A stock. Class A stock carries more voting rights than Class B.

Use Your Personal Knowledge

A good place to start in deciding which companies to research is to use your own areas of expertise to guide you. If you're a real estate agent, start researching real estate companies. If you're a car collector, look at automobile stocks. You'll have to branch out from there obviously (remember diversification!) but starting there will let you get your feet wet in an industry where you're comfortable with the language and understand the underlying asset.

A. Find Companies To Research

The market is crowded in almost every area, and it's not possible to research every company. Look for a handful of stocks that look appealing, and focus your energies there. Analysts can be helpful here, but be sure to look for analysts with styles and motivations that mirror your own. An aggressive risk taker's recommendations won't be of much use to you if you're more cautious. Stock screener websites are another wonderful resource. These sites compile some of the relevant data about thousands of stocks and allow you to sort by industry, price, and a lot of other factors.

You can as well know about good companies to invest in by listening to some experts or reading helpful commentaries about them. If you are watching CNBC, CNN Money, and other business segments of popular TV stations, you will hear experts and investors talk about the pros and cons of putting their money in some companies.

However, consider this important warning: You are not expected to just follow the crowd to do stock investing, you should go ahead and do your own research and analysis before finally making up your mind on where to put your money.

Another yardstick some investors use in selecting a company is to go to where they think the management is solid. Though there may be no concrete evidence to prove this, when Steve Job, a reliable technocrat and leader, was at the helms of Apple, Inc., there were some investors who put their money into the company because of him. This can be confirmed in the event that followed his death when some long-time Apple investors started to slice down the amount of their investment in the company.

So, if there is any CEO you have heard great stories about and, to some extent, you are sure of his/her wonderful leadership to steer the company towards constant profitability, you may want to take a look at the company for possible investment. This should just be an eye-opener for you because it is still imperative to do extra research on the company. Have you ever wondered why a company's share goes up or down when there is a change of leadership? It is because when a terrible CEO is replaced, the company's share will soar; but when a good CEO departs due to irreconcilable differences with the company's board of directors, the price of the company's share will go down.

B. Examine Fundamentals, Not Stock Histories

As briefly explained above, you need to go very deep in investigating the fundamentals of the company you are hoping to invest in. Looking at the performance of a stock is not enough! You need to look at the company itself. How are its revenues? What profits are they reporting? Is there anything that sets it apart from the competition? How much debt does it hold? How do these factors compare to other companies in the same industry? Also, make sure to look at the management. High turnover, mass exoduses, and inconsistent visions for the company are all warning signs. Look for boards with a stable lineup and a clear mission with a solid plan to achieve it.

All these precautions are necessary to help you invest wisely and not throw your hard-earned money into the abyss. As a matter of fact, run away from the company that have the following problems:

- ***Poor management structure***: Any company with poor and disorderly management structure is not worthy of your investment. This is because, sooner or later, the irreconcilable differences among its executive officers will soon spill over to the company's performance and reduce its share value. Well, you may want to ask: How can I know a company that has this problem? Of course, you can! If you have been following the news about that particular company, you would have read in the newspapers about the management issues faced by the company. When its chairman is always quarreling with its CEO and other senior executives, that is a warning sign that the company is about to implode. Many companies have fallen apart due to this major problem, and those who will suffer from this matter are the investors.

- *No hope of profitability*: When you notice a company that has been operating in the red for several years and has no hope of turning black any time soon, run away! It is true that most companies don't turn profitable within a few years of operation; however, when a company stays unprofitable for so many years, it seems something is wrong with its management and cost of operations. That means that if you put your money into such a company, you may not receive dividends quite soon, and your investment in its stock may decline any time from the moment.
- *Short shelf-life of products/services*: If the company you are planning to invest in does not have products/services that people will love to buy in the long-term, don't throw your money in the garbage can. The value of a company increases or decreases based on the overall quality and usefulness of its products/services. So,

also your investment. This is why the concept of value investing is important. When you bought a company's stock, you are becoming a partner or a part-owner; and if its products or services are great and bringing good revenues, that will also be passed to you through your investment.

- ***Micro – and Macro – economic impacts***: Make sure you are investing in company that can stand both micro- and macro-economic challenges. Do not invest in a company that will collapse when there is a sudden economic or financial crisis. You can know more about a company's financial strength through their annual report or other independent reports about it. Many investors have lost their money in weak companies that die all of a sudden because they don't have buffers to withstand an unexpected financial crisis.

Choosing a Broker

A broker is someone licensed to buy and sell stocks (and other instruments) on exchanges on your behalf. There are several types, ranging from Full Service Brokers to Discount Brokers. With the former, you'll receive comprehensive financial advice, accounting, and tax guidance in addition to having someone execute your trades. The latter is only going to make trades and execute orders for you. Brokers charge a fee, whether per trade or per share traded, and as I'm sure you can imagine the full-service broker is going to charge a much higher fee. Choosing one will depend on a few factors, such as the amount you have to invest, how complicated or straightforward the investments are, and how many trades you anticipate making per quarter.

Keep in mind that some companies allow their stock to be bought directly. If that's something you're interested in, you can usually find that information on their website. If not, give them a call and ask.

Here are 7 characteristics of a good broker:

(i)   ***Reasonable commission and margin rates***: The primary reason for investing in stocks is to make profits or gains. So, if your broker charges high fees and low margin rates. Normally, full-service brokers such as Merrill Lynch, Bank of America, Morgan Stanley, and Wells Fargo charge as high as $100 per trade, which is roughly 1% to 2% of the trade size. These kinds of high-fee brokers are good for institutional investors or millionaires. If you want to buy stocks as a rookie investor, it is advisable that you utilize the services of low-cost brokers such as Interactive Brokers, which charges $0.005 per share and has a margin rate of 1.59%. In the same way, Lightspeed (another broker) can execute your trade for $0.0045 per share and it has a margin rate of 6%.

(ii) ***Free Mutual fund and ETF trading***: To reduce the cost of trading, you should go for a broker that offers free ETF and Mutual Fund trading. Take for instance, Charles Schwab and Fidelity have the cheapest rates (zero rate) for some broad-based ETFs. Though these two brokers charge more than either Interactive Brokers or Lightspeed.

(iii) ***Useful trading tools***: To succeed as a stock investor, you must have at your disposal some useful trading tools. The kinds of tools available to stock traders vary from one broker to another. For examples, these tools include trading platforms or systems, back-testing systems, demo-trading system, portfolio-review tool, and fixed-income investing tool. If your broker isn't providing the right tools you need to succeed in your trading, leave!

(iv) ***Stock options***: Embrace a broker that also provides an opportunity to trade stock options. This will give you another chance to make more money. Who knows if stock option will turn out to be the easiest way to make a lot of money as an investor.

(v) ***Foreign stocks***: Make sure your broker can give you access to foreign stocks. More than half of the world's stock markets are outside the United States. Since many foreign companies are not listed on U.S. exchange, you must be able to buy their stocks through your broker. This is a good way to diversify your investments. Brokers such as Interactive Brokers, E * Trade, and EverTrade provide opportunities for their clients to trade in foreign stocks.

(vi) ***How about dividend reinvestment?*** If you are going to be a long-term investor, it is advisable you sign up with a broker that offers dividend reinvestment. In this way, your dividends will be automatically reinvested. You wouldn't need to pay extra commissions on the reinvested dividends. If you have chosen to withdraw your dividends and plan to manually invest them, you will lose some money to commissions.

(vii) ***Investment research and banking services***: It is also imperative that your broker offers some forms of investment research and banking services. Stock investing is not a monolithic process, it involves series of investment research before you can arrive at a winning strategy. Your broker must supply both fundamental and technical analyses and make available tools you can use in researching companies and their stock values. Similarly, if your broker doesn't provide smooth banking services, which will facilitate the process of depositing and withdrawing money from your account, you may end up paying a lot for transaction costs. Bank charges may bite deeper into your profits if you are an institutional or millionaire investor. But when your broker provides a smooth avenue to deposit and withdraw funds from your account, you won't have to be bothered about paying huge bank transfer charges.

Apart from the great attributes of a stock broker mentioned above, it is also good to have a broker that offers multi-lingual platforms. For example, if you are bilingual, say you speak French and English, having your trading platforms in both languages may enrich your stock investing experience. In the same way, the trading platforms must be customizable, meaning you can design or arrange the interface the way you like. This will give you a comfortable feeling as you concentrate on your stock trading.

Tracking Your Income

Eventually, you'll have to pay taxes on this income, and if you have losses, they need to be accounted for too. Because gains are not always straightforward, it's important to keep careful track of every trade you make. There are different ways to calculate how much a particular stock has earned or lost you over a given time, so you'll need as much information as possible to share with your accountant at tax time. Most trading platforms or systems have an accounting section where you can keep track of your gains, losses and overall balance. In some cases, you may need to print them and present to your accountants for tax and other purposes.

It is disturbing to realize that some investors think that stock trading isn't a taxable activity. This is absolutely untrue. If you have made some gains in your investments, you must appropriately record them on your tax papers. The worse issue is that you can't hide them from the IRS; this is because your broker, if it is based in the United States, has an obligation to report its activities to the U.S. Securities and

Exchange Commission. In this case, you may be exposed and charged for tax evasion by the IRS.

Outlined below are four steps you can adopt in being accountable in your stock trading:

- Keep a daily or weekly report of your trading activities. You can record, in a file, your daily or weekly gains and losses. If you don't want to do it this way, you can print your daily or weekly report from your trading platform or system
- Know all your tax responsibilities, as far as stock trading is concerned. Find out what you need to do when you incurred some losses. And know how much taxes you will be paying on your capital gains or dividends. Understand that the tax rate may be different from one state to another
- Use a broker that also exhibits a high-level of accountability. This is very important so that you can always have back-up accounting information in case you need to make a reference to it in the near future. If a broker is unaccountable in most of its practices, avoid it.
- If you don't know how to handle your trading finances, you can hire an accountant to do that for you. An experienced security

accountant knows exactly what to do to help you get your financial accountability in shape.

Chapter 5. Alternative Investment Options

Stock investing is not a holistic process in itself, it is connected with other forms of investment that you can get involved in so as to increase your overall gains or returns. This section looks carefully into other investment options you can engage in. Remember that the most important thing is that you will be able to diversify your portfolio for the purpose of safety and better earnings. If you are going to be an active manager of your investments, the following alternative investment options will give you

Hedge Funds

A hedge fund is an alternative investment vehicle mostly available to experienced and sophisticated investors, like institutions and individuals with huge assets or investment capital.

Like mutual funds, hedge funds are pools of underlying securities, and they can be invested in many types of securities.

However, there are some differences between these two investment vehicles.

- Hedge funds are not, at the moment, regulated by the U.S. Securities and Exchange Commission (SEC).

- By not being regulated, hedge funds can invest in a wider range of securities than mutual funds can.

- Because many hedge funds do invest in traditional securities like stocks, bonds, commodities and real estate, they are best known for using really sophisticated and risky investment techniques.

- Hedge funds normally use long-short strategies, which indicates that hedge fund managers typically invest in some balance of long positions and short positions.

- Likewise, many hedge funds invest in "derivatives," which are contracts to buy or sell another security at a specified price.

- Many hedge funds also utilize an investment technique called leverage, which is actually investing with borrowed money, a strategy that could significantly increase potential rewards.

- Hedge funds are typically not as liquid as mutual funds, which means that it is more difficult to sell your shares. Mutual funds have a per-share price (called a net asset value) that is calculated each day, so you could sell your shares at any time.

- Most hedge funds seem to generate returns over a specific period of time called a "lockup period," when investors cannot sell their shares.

- Hedge fund managers are also compensated differently from mutual fund managers. Mutual fund managers are paid fees irrespective of their funds' performance. Hedge fund managers, on the other hand, receive a percentage of the returns they earn for investors, in addition to collecting a "management fee" that ranges anyway from 1% to 4% of the net asset value of the fund.

Investing in REITs

Real Estate Investment Trust - is a type of security that invests in real estate via property or mortgages and it is often traded on major exchanges like a stock. REITs offer investors with an extremely liquid stake in real estate. They will receive special tax considerations and normally offer high dividend yields.
Irrespective of their ages, individual investors in the U.S. and worldwide can invest in REITs directly or through REIT mutual funds. Other known buyers of REITs are pension funds, exchange traded

funds, endowments, insurance companies, foundations, and bank trust departments.

The main reasons investors are attracted to REITs are their high levels of recurrent income and the opportunity for long-term growth. Today, a broad range of investors are using REITs to maintain financial stability. With REITs, you can also achieve the investment goals of diversification, liquidity, dividends, transparency, and performance.

Why you should invest in REITs

REITs can guarantee total returns for an investment. You can typically earn high dividends and achieve the potential for moderate, long-term capital appreciation. It is generally believed that the long-term total returns of REIT stocks may be less than the returns of higher risk, high-growth stocks but somehow more than the returns of lower risk bonds.

The law expects REITs to distribute to their shareholders at least 90 percent of their taxable income each year. Hence, REITs become one of those companies paying the highest dividends to investors. The dividends come mainly from the predominantly stable and predictable stream of contractual rents paid by the tenants who occupy the REIT's properties. Since rental rates appear to go up during periods of inflation, the good news is that REIT dividends are protected from the long-term destructive effect of rising prices.

You can notice that the low correlation of listed REIT stock returns with the returns of other equities and fixed-income investments varies over time. This is why it is important to include listed REITs in your investment program so as to build a more diversified portfolio.

If you are investing in REITs, these are the benefits you will get:

- **Income & Long-term Growth**
- **High Dividend Yield**
- **Liquidity**

To achieve this, you need an effective professional management to help you look after your REITs. To carry out the oversight of your investments, there are independent directors of the REIT, independent auditors, independent analysts, and the business and financial media that typically monitor a publicly traded REIT's financial reporting from time to time. This scrutiny is essential so as to guarantee accountability in the process and provide investors with some protection.

If your REITs are registered with the U.S. Securities and Exchange Commission (SEC), you are expected to make regular SEC disclosures, which include quarterly and yearly financial reports. These procedures are necessary to create an environment of safety and reliability.

Venture Capital Investing

Venture capital (VC) is a kind of private equity, which is a form of financing provided by firms or funds to small, emerging firms that appeared to have high growth potential, or which have demonstrated commendable high growth as shown in the number of employees, annual revenue, or both.

Venture capital firms or funds put their money in these early-stage companies in exchange for equity (an ownership stake) in the companies they are investing in. Instead of buying shares directly from the small firms, their equity in them automatically award some amount of stocks to them.

As a venture capitalist, you are taking on the risk of financing risky start-ups with the expectation that some of the firms you funded will become successful. Most of these start-ups that sought funding are usually based on an innovative technology or business model. And they are mostly from the high technology industries, such as information technology (IT), pharmaceutical, biotechnology, and social media.

It is advisable that you should make your venture capital investment after an initial "seed funding" round. This is after the start-up has obtained initial funding from sources that may include their friends, relatives, small bank loans, or grants. Thus, the first round of institutional venture capital to fund growth is called the Series A round. Other series are code-named series B, C, and so on.

As a venture capitalist, you are providing this financing with the hope of generating a return through an "exit" event. An exit strategy means once the start-up begins to be profitable, you may liquidate your equity in it by selling your shares to the public for the first time in an Initial public offering (IPO) or doing a merger and acquisition of the company.

Why venture capital investment is popular?

Venture capital is very helpful to new companies that urgently need some funding to expand their operations, or hire new employees.

These companies cannot secure financing from other sources because—

- They have limited operating history, maybe they are newly incorporated and have no industry-wide experience.
- They are too small to raise capital in the public markets
- They have not reached the point where they are able to secure a bank loan
- They are not developed enough to apply for a debt offering or issue a bond

There are plenty of risks to undertake as a venture capitalist, because you can never guarantee that the start-ups you are supporting can succeed. However, in exchange for the high risk you assume by investing in smaller and early-stage companies, you can have some control over the company decisions and own a significant portion of the companies' ownership.

The good news is that start-ups like Uber, Facebook, Airbnb, Flipkart, and Alibaba are highly valued startups that received venture capitalists' money when they were growing. Today, those venture capitalists will be happy for making such an investment, because they can reap their efforts in many folds, commensurate with their level of investment.

Private equities

Private equity is a way to invest in some asset that isn't publicly traded, or to invest in a publicly traded asset with the intention of taking it private.

On the other hand, venture capital invests in private companies with the intention to keep private or make it public. And Unlike stocks, bonds, and mutual funds, private equity funds usually invest in more illiquid assets, that is, companies. By purchasing companies, the firms gain access to those companies' assets and revenue sources, which can lead to very high returns on investments.

Commodities

A commodity can be a basic good used in commerce that is interchangeable with other commodities of the same type;

commodities are most often used as inputs in the production of other goods or services. The quality of a given commodity may differ slightly, but it is essentially uniform across producers. When commodities are traded on an exchange, they

features of a given product may be completely different depending on the producer.

You can invest in a commodity company by buying their shares or you can purchase the commodities yourself and sell them. Some traditional examples of commodities include oil, coffee, cotton, grains, gold, beef, and natural gas. However, the definition of commodity has expanded to include financial products like foreign currencies and indexes, cell phone minutes and bandwidth

You should understand that the sale and purchase of commodities is usually carried out through futures contracts on exchanges which standardize the quantity and minimum quality of the commodity being traded. For instance, the Chicago Board of Trade that one wheat contract is for 5,000 bushels and also lists what grades of wheat can be used to satisfy the contract.

There are two types of traders that trade commodity futures. The first are actual buyers and producers/sellers of commodities that use commodity futures contracts to hedge against the purposes for which the commodities were initially intended. Theses traders purchase and take delivery of the actual commodity when the futures contract expires. Take for instance, the wheat farmer that plants a crop can hedge against the risk of losing money if the price of wheat falls just before the crop is harvested. The farmer can sell wheat futures contracts when the crop is planted and can receive a guaranteed price for the wheat at the time it is harvested.

The second group of commodities trader is the speculator. This category of traders is those who trade in the commodities markets for the purpose of profiting from the volatile price movements. They never had any plan to buy or take delivery of the actual commodity when the futures contract expires.

It is interesting that many of the futures markets are very liquid; they have a high degree of daily range and volatility. This is why they are very tempting markets for intraday traders. Many of the index futures are used by brokerages and portfolio managers to offset risk. Also, since commodities do not typically trade in tandem with equity and bond markets, they can also be used effectively to diversify an investment portfolio.

Chapter 6. Glossary

Annual Report- A document that contains a company's full financial information. The SEC requires every publicly traded company to file several financial reports; the Annual Report is the distillation of those documents.

Blue Chip Stock- Also known as "bellwether" stocks, these are the stocks of big, usually old, companies that are well respected and highly regarded.

Broker- is an individual person who arranges transactions between a buyer and a seller for a commission when the deal is successfully executed. A stock broker facilitates the buying and selling of stocks between the investors and the exchange or companies.

Commodities -are a basic good used in commerce that is interchangeable with other commodities of the same type. They are most often used as inputs in the production of other goods or services and they include examples like gold, silver, copper, oil, coffee, cotton, metals, gas, and so on.

Dividend- The portion of a company's profits that are distributed to the shareholders.

Diversification - Diversification is a risk management tool that combines many investments within a portfolio. The idea behind this technique is that a portfolio that is made up of different kinds of investments will, on average, yield higher returns and face a lower risk than any individual investment found within the portfolio.

DRIPs - A dividend reinvestment plan (DRIP) is provided by a corporation that permits investors to reinvest all or part of their cash dividends by buying additional shares or fractional shares on the dividend payment date. A DRIP is a good way to increase the value of your investment. Most DRIPs give investors the chance to buy shares commission-free and at a good discount to the current share price, but do not permit reinvestments that is much lower than $10.

ETFs - exchange traded funds, are a marketable security that tracks an index, a commodity, bonds, or a basket of assets like an index fund.

However, unlike mutual funds, ETFs trade like a common stock on a stock exchange. ETFs can experience price changes throughout the day as they are bought and sold. ETFs usually have higher daily liquidity and lower fees than mutual fund shares – that is why they are attractive alternative for individual investors.

Equities- Investments represent partial ownership of a company. Stocks are a very common example of an equity.

Foreign stocks – are all stocks of non-U.S. companies. Many of these foreign stocks are not available on U.S. exchanges. So, to purchase them, you must sign up with a broker that has the connection to trade these stocks on their platforms. For example, Interactive Brokers allows its customers to deal in foreign stocks.

Fundamental Analysis – In stock trading, fundamental analysis is a technique that investors use to determine a security's value by concentrating on the underlying factors that affect a company's *main* business activities and future prospects. Generally, you can perform fundamental analysis on industries or the economy.

The term simply denotes the analysis of the economic well-being of a financial entity and not only its price movements.

Growth Stock - is a share in a company whose earnings are projected to grow at an above-average rate relative to the market. A good company with a wonderful product or service has the tendency to grow exponentially, so as the value of its stock.

Hedge Funds - are alternative investment options that use pooled funds and employ different strategies to earn active return, or alpha, for their investors. Hedge funds could be managed aggressively or consist of derivatives and leverage in both domestic and international markets for the purpose of generating high returns.

LEAPs - Long-term equity anticipation securities (LEAPs) are publicly traded options contracts which have expiration dates that are more than one year. LEAPS are not different from short-term options, but the LEAPs' expiration dates provide the opportunity for long-term investors to gain exposure to sustained price changes without the need to execute a combination of shorter-term option contracts.

Limit Order- A directive given to a broker that sets a price limit on shares, above which the share will not be purchased.

Market Order- This is a simple order directing a broker to buy or sell a specified amount of shares at the market price.

Mutual Funds - is an investment process comprising of a pool of funds collected from many investors for the aim of investing in securities like stocks, bonds, money market instruments and similar assets. Mutual funds are operated by money managers, who invest the fund's capital in order to produce capital gains and income for the fund's investors. A mutual fund's portfolio is organized and sustained to fulfil the investment objectives stated in its prospectus.

Options- These are contracts that represent the right, but not the obligation, to buy or sell shares for a specific period of time for a specific price.

Put options - is an option contract that gives the owner the right, but not the obligation, to sell a specified amount of an underlying security at a particular price within a specified time. This is the direct opposite of a call option, which allows the holder the right to buy shares.

REIT - Real Estate Investment Trust - is a type of security that invests in real estate via property or mortgages and it is often traded on major exchanges like a stock. REITs offer investors with an extremely liquid stake in real estate. They will receive special tax considerations and normally offer high dividend yields.

SEC - The **U.S. Securities and Exchange Commission (SEC)** is an agency of the United States federal government. Its main responsibility is to enforce the federal securities laws, propose securities rules, and regulate the securities industry, the nation's stock and options exchanges, and other activities and organizations, including the electronic securities markets in the United States.

Short Selling - Short selling can be defined as the sale of a security that is not owned by the seller, or the security that the seller has borrowed. Short selling is encouraged by the concept that a security's price will decline, enabling it to be bought back at a cheaper price to make a tangible profit.

Stop Order- Also called a stop loss, this is a directive for a broker to immediately sell shares which drop below a specified price.

Technical Analysis - Technical analysis is a trading tool used in evaluating securities in order to forecast their future movement by analyzing statistics collected from trading activity, like price movement and volume. In contrast with the fundamental analysts who try to evaluate a security's intrinsic value, technical analysts concentrate on charts of price movement and various analytical tools to determine a security's strength or weakness and then forecast future price changes.

Trading platform - A trading platform is a software by which investors and traders can open, close and manage their market positions. Trading platforms are normally provided by brokers for free or at a discount rate in exchange for keeping a funded account and/or making a particular number of trades per month.

Value stocks - is a stock that trades at a lower price relative to its fundamentals (for examples, dividends, earnings and sales) and have been undervalued by a value investor. Because they are cheap stocks, their value increases over a long period of time. So, value investors purchased and held them for many years.

Postscript

The stock market has a reputation for volatility, but hopefully, now you understand how to mitigate risk and invest in a safer, more secure way. While the movies and legends give attention to the high-stakes, high-speed traders who make or lose fortunes, the stock market is mostly populated with calculated risks and steady hands. Knowing this, and treating stocks as the long-term investments they out to be is the key to success. Don't forget to do your homework too! As famed investor Warren Buffett put it, "Risk comes from not knowing what you're doing." Arming yourself with knowledge, tempering your emotions with facts, and developing a plan for your financial future set you up for a great future as an investor.

The psychology of a successful stock trader

It is not enough to know the different types of investments you can do as an individual investor, the most important thing is to know yourself. This is because not all investment types will be good for you. Some risks may be too high for you to handle. And you may have the natural habit of responding to losses poorly. In order to be a sane and successful trader, these psychological tips may help you:

- Never trade in an amount that is psychologically too big for you. For example, if you are comfortable with buying 100 shares, do so. Don't think that because you have got the money and invested in 1000 shares of a company. The downside is that when the share value starts to drop, you may find yourself losing it mentally. Many traders have ended up being depressed because of taking too much risk that they are not psychologically prepared for.
- Celebrate every gain or reward that you get. This will give you some boost as you move to your next trade
- Don't lose your mind over a lost trade. In fact, losing is part of the game of stock investing
- Never compete with anyone on trading, except you are in a stock trading competition. Each trader is unique in his/her own way
- Do not imitate people's trading strategy. While it is helpful to learn from the others, do your own fundamental and technical analyses before deciding on what trade to make
- Have a clear vision of which trade you will like to make—this is almost like visualizing the outcome of the trade before taking it.
- Having a positive outlook on trades can also lead to better outcomes. This means that when you are about to execute a trade,

you must be sure of your expected outcome. If in doubt, it is better to stay put and do nothing.

- Do not over trade! You won't like yourself being stressed out, both mentally and physically. This could take a great toll on your ability to think through a trade. Most traders use their discretions to carry out a trade, but when your mind is already blank from exhaustion or stress, you won't be able to plan properly

- When in a problem, always seek some help from experienced stock traders. One of the main reasons bank and institutional traders lose a lot of money is that they make virtually most of their decisions by themselves, without running them through their superiors.

How to become a better trader or investor

If you can painstakingly follow these 6 strategies, you can become a better stock trader or investor. Some of these techniques may not be new to you, but they are the essential tools or processes used by many profitable stock investors:

1. ***Trading time***: Over time, you will discover the best time for your trades. There are four distinct trading hours: They are Sydney, Tokyo, London, and New York trading sessions. Even though you can engage in stock trading for 24 hours, each of

the trading zones listed above starts at a particular time. If you are aiming to buy some shares from a British company, you would have to wait until the FTSE opens for business in London. In the same way, if you think of purchasing some Japanese stocks, you must wait until Nikkei opens for business. Apart from knowing the different trading times, traders have some peculiar times when they are most likely to score a win. If you have been trading for some time you would have discovered when exactly is the right time for you to enter a trade and exit with some encouraging gains.

2. **Careful leveraging**: You need a leverage to increase your chance of making more gains in your investment. With a buy on 40% or 50% margin can almost double your investment if the share price goes up. In this case, you are purchasing a stock with half its worth. But you must do this very carefully. Because if the same stock price falls like 20%, you are going to incur a loss totaled your initial investment. As a matter of fact, leveraging is both a blessing and a curse, depending on how you play the game.

3. **Do the right analysis**: It doesn't matter how many trading tools you have on your trading platform: All that is important is that

you know and use the ones that can give you the right analysis. The two major analyses you can use as a trader are fundamental and technical analyses. So, the question is which tools do you use to get your analyses? While some traders prefer Moving Average (MA) as their sole or main technical tool, others may add other tools such as Relative Strength Index (RSI), Bollinger Bands, MACD, and so on to it. Similar, the source of fundamental analysis for many stock traders are the company's annual reports, earning releases, news, and investors' manuals. You may not have to use all these tools to obtain your analysis. So, try to be specific with the ones that have worked for you in the past. The most important thing is the reliability of your analysis, not the amount of analyses you had done.

4. ***Great money management***: Knowing how to manage your investment capital is as important as understanding any trading strategy. It doesn't matter if you are a professional trader or a newbie, if you can't simply protect your investment you will soon be stopped and kicked out of your investment. Money management, in stock trading, entails knowing how many shares of a company to buy, which amount to invest in bonds,

mutual funds, or hedge funds. When you are doing your diversification, you must make sure it has a reference to how smartly you need to use your investment capital. If care is not taken, you may end up losing some or all of your money. Applying the appropriate leverage is also part of money management. If you purchased a stock on a high margin, any slight downside may throw you into a huge loss!

5. *Winning mindset*: This is somehow related to the psychology of a successful trader described above. To win in life, whether as a trader or wrestler, you must have a winning mindset. That does not mean you must be over-ambitious and take to many risks. Stock trading is a delicate process, and the best approach to winning at this game is to do everything with caution and deliberation. As a discretionary trader, you must make sure that the shots you are calling are right and success-oriented. There are no guarantees that the trades you are making will be profitable. And there is no better way to increase the chance of winning than being very optimistic, while reducing the extent of errors and mistakes that newbie often make.

6. *Experience*: In every human endeavor, experience is the most essential ingredient that can necessitate success. In other

words, the more experienced you are as a trader, the better your overall performance will be. If you are someone who is new to stock trading, you don't need to be scared of participating in stock trading. All you should do is to get some education about how the whole stock trading process work. There are three different ways you can obtain the appropriate knowledge about stock trading:

- Seeing what other experienced traders are doing. The idea is not for you to copy their trades, but to see the way they do it. It is more or less like apprenticing—no other fastest way to learn than seeing what the "masters" in the game are doing
- Online education about stock trading can also help you a lot. Some of them are free and offer free resources you can consult every now and then.
- Learning by trial and error—this is the most dangerous one. And wasteful, too. There are going to be a lot of losses before you can get confident on trading stock. The best thing you can do is to demo-trade. Every broker provides the opportunity to demo a trade on their platforms. Your performance on demo trading will give you the confidence to graduate into real-money trading.

www.ingramcontent.com/pod-product-compliance
Lightning Source LLC
Chambersburg PA
CBHW070106210526
45170CB00013B/763